HEALING AND REGENERATION THROUGH MUSIC

By
CORINNE HELINE

A companion study to
Healing and Regeneration Through Color
by the same author

DeVorss & Co., *Publishers*
P.O. Box 550
Marina Del Rey, CA 90291

IN THIS VOLUME
The Music of the Spheres
Music and the Prenatal Life
Music of the Zodiac in Relation to the Human Body
Healing and Music
Music as a Healing Agent for Insanity
Keynotes of Master Musicians
Regeneration Through Music
A New World Music

Nineteenth Edition 1980

ISBN: 0-87516-431-5

Printed in the United States of America by
Book Graphics, Inc., Marina Del Rey, CA 90291

Cover Art copyright 1978 by Promotive Healthing.

The Music of the Spheres

The entire world is a musical instrument, the pole of the world celestial is intersected where this heavenly chord is divided by the spiritual sun. Earthly music is an echo of this cosmic harmony; it is a relic of heaven.

—Author unknown.

THE processes of creation or construction are all dependent upon the vibrational power of tone. "The universe is builded to music," said the Kabbalists.

The Ageless Wisdom teaches that when the One entered into manifestation Its emanating powers were twelve in number. At a later stage these twelve were resolved into seven. Hence, seven has become the tonal key of the finite or concrete universe, while twelve remains as the original or initial symphonic outflow of Deity. This first great musical outpouring was given verbal expression when God said, "Let there be light."

The numerical power of twelve is the highest spiriutal emanation active in the universe, and seven transforms that power into the concreting and building forces that operate on the physical plane.

The twelve semitones of the chromatic scale and the seven notes of the diatonic are numeric divisions corresponding to the cosmic pattern of the zodiac and our solar system, respectively. In our immediate cosmic environment, the twelve zodiacal constellations serve as the sounding board for the music played by the seven planets native to our solar system as they circle around their parent sun. Socrates, in a poetic description of this phenomenon, declares that "On the upper surface of each circle is a siren who goes round with it humming a single note which all together forms one great harmony."

Shakespeare, too, sings of this celestial music:

> *There's not the smallest orb which thou beholdest,*
> *But in his motion like an angel sings,*
> *Still quiring to the young eyed cherubins;*
> *Such harmony is in immortal souls,*
> *But whilst this muddy vesture of decay*
> *Doth grossly close it in, we cannot hear it.*

A study of the symphonic aspect of the cosmic pattern and its relation to musical science as we know it offers not only an absorbingly fascinating field for occult investigation but also the key to great power, capable of practical application that goes far to remove in our consciousness the sense of separateness that now exists between the seen and the unseen, the material and the spiritual. When the fact of universal inter-relationship becomes a living truth in our consciousness we truly know ourselves as a part of that One "in whom we live and move and have our being."

In the musical laws underlying creation the twelve semitones of the chromatic scale sound the initial music of the twelve zodiacal Hierarchies, and the seven notes of the diatonic scale transmit the key tones of the seven Spirits before the Throne of God, or the seven planets of this solar system.

It was on the number seven that Pythagoras, the generally accredited discoverer of the diatonic scale, evolved the doctrine of the music of the spheres. According to his calculations the distance from the Moon to the Earth corresponded to one tone; the distance from the Moon to Mercury equalled a semitone; from Mercury to Venus one and one-half tones; Sun to Mars one tone; Mars to Jupiter, a semitone; Jupiter to Saturn, a semitone; and Saturn to the fixed stars, or zodiac, one and one-half tones.

Musical science is based upon the fundamental principle of the rhythms of the universe. Since these rhythms preceded the manifestation of cosmos, the latter being built upon them, it follows that music emerged with the very first breath of divine creation. This music, being the first of the arts, shall also be the last, the alpha and the omega, the highest and the most important of them all.

The tonal patterns of Twelve, Seven, and Five as expressed in the chromatic and diatonic scales are fundamental to the universal structure of things. This being true, it is to be expected that these same numerical patterns hsould appear again and again throughout all nature. And so they do, as common observation readily verifies.

On the musical keyboard five dark keys and seven white keys make up the octave. Corresponding to this are the seven "globes" upon which evolution is carried forward during each of the seven creative days and the five "globes" over which it proceeds during each of the intervening cosmic nights. It is also in keeping with this evolutionary pattern that the spectrum shows seven colors which are seen with ordinary sight as clear as "day," but with five more colors discernible only to etheric vision, or the sight that sees even in the dark of night.

Occultism reveals a similar correspondence in humanity's relation to the twelve creative Hierarchies. Seven are active in helping man to progress upon his path, whereas five have completed their work with humanity and withdrawn to higher planes of being.

The forces of the Twelve are cosmic; they are basic and all-inclusive. In the present stage of evolution mankind can but sense the nature of their operations. Only the Illuminati are able to comprehend and interpret the full workings of the twelve-fold force. The Seven, however, reduce and re-channel the forces of the Twelve to the point of physical concretion in which material form becomes visible and audible to human perception.

The Five operate during the mystic intervals between the Days and work with the process by which the vibrational rhythms of objective activity are lowered so as to be made suitable for the subjective activity of assimilation which proceeds during the cosmic nights.

From this fact we may discover by analogy that the world work of the Five is to bring forth into active manifestation the forces that gestate in silence and darkness during the night time, even as the seed when buried in the ground puts forth latent powers in the form of new life. The mystic intervals of rest and assimilation between the days of objective activity are spoken of as nights because they are without the light that accompanies outer manifestation. This is why black symbolizes spiritual power in latency as white represents the same power in manifestation.

Major tones create objectively and minor tones build subjectively. As man works consciously in the outer world under the impulses of the major notes, so also does he work subjectively on the inner planes in developing and expanding his faculties under the influence of the minor tones.

The major keys (scales) are outpouring, productive, expanding; the minor keys (scales) are secretive, sustaining, enfolding.

In the annual cycle of seasons, the earth alternates periodically between two rhythmic moods, a major and a minor. At the Autumn Equinox it changes from the major tones that have dominated during spring and summer to the minors that prevail during autumn and winter.

It is through a blending of positive and negative forces in nature, or a combination of the masculine and feminine potencies, that the hidden energies become externalized in visible form. In musical scales we may observe such a blend between the feminine flats and the masculine sharps. In that blend there are always seven tones involved. To illustrate: The forces projected through one flat bear the feminine modulation that occurs in a masculine pitch in six sharps. Two flats concur with five sharps, three flats with four sharps, four flats with three sharps, five flats with two sharps, and six flats with one sharp. Thus we see that the musical gamut audible to the physical ear is measured by seven.

The keyboard of the piano is composed of eighty-eight keys, which number reduces numeralogically to seven. It is also significant to note that the number seven is composed of the numerals three and four, three being masculine and representative of the powers of spirit and four being feminine and representative of the potencies of matter. the supreme purpose of the sevenfold evolutionary era is the transmutation of matter into

The Music of the Spheres

spirit.

Every sound emanates a certain color and takes on a definite form. Conversely, every form gives forth a sound; that sound is its keynote. Every created thing, from molecule to man and from plant to solar system, possesses a keynote of its own. The sum total of all these notes makes up the music of the spheres.

"The musical character of the universe is sensed by the clairvoyant," writes C. Jinarajadasa in *First Principles of Theosophy*. Amplifying the statement he continues: "As rhythm in structure and movement means music, the universe makes music as it works at its tasks. The electrons make waves as they rush through the aether, but their notes are scarcely within the audibility of the average clairaudient ear. But the note which the earth makes as it circles the sun, pushing its way thorugh the aether, and the harmonies of that note can be heard. Each visible and invisible planet has its note, and the music of the spheres is not a fantasy but a most sober verity."

A few years ago there was perfected in Germany a delicate instrument by which it was possible to hear the sound of growing grass. To those whose hearing has been raised to the etheric octave, this sound may be heard without the aid of a physical mechanism. To the clairaudient person nature in all her manifold forms is literally heard performing a symphony of divine sublimity. Flowers, trees, and grasses—every growing thing—come into being and maintain their existence in harmony with symphonic patterns of sound that are indescribably beautiful. The winds are tuned to certain rhythms, as is also the beat of the waves. The tides also have their rhythm, coming in on majors and going out in minors. The combined sounds of everything on earth compose a harmonic chord which is the keynote of our planet. It is in the key of F whose tone becomes visible as green, and is, therefore, earth's basic color note.

Every organ of man's body-temple has been fashioned by the creative rhythms of the starry Hierarchies. The beating of the heart, the flow of the blood, the play of the muscles, the pulsations of the breath are all a part of this great body-symphony, and echo, faintly though it be, the sublime music of the spheres.

Max Heindel, a Rosicrucian Inititate, in his instructions to students of astro-diagnosis states that in health the vital body emits a sound which is continuous and very like the hum of a bumblebee. Blended with this sound there is also to be heard the swift motion of the vital fluid which flows through the body and emanates an auric radiance.

In health the keynote of the vital body is always in harmony with the keynote of the archetype. As a result of a generally increasing refinement of perception, due to the growing influence of the Aquarian and Uranian rays in the new zodiacal cycle now opening, material science is corroborating these occult truths by laboratory experimentation. The report in the *Canadian Theosophist* of a lecture delivered by Dr. Yngve Zotterman, a Swedish physiologist at the University of Toronto, is in point. According to this savant, nerve sensations could be recorded on a gramaphone record, broadcast, and even projected on the screen. "A recording of the ordinary impulses of a nerve in the hand," reads the report, "sounded like wireless atmospherics, but more regular." Cotton being drawn across the hand produced a noise like hail-stones falling on a tin roof. Much the same effect was heard when a stick of wood was used, and, in addition, a noise like the slow roll of a kettledrum which continued for a little time afterwards and which the doctor said was the effect of pain, explaining that "pain and certain emotions are carried by the thinner fibres and the impulses continue after the first sharp pain is over." A regular rattling noise and sounds as of sharp pistol-shots were the result of cold water being placed upon the tongue, while the throbbing pain of a burn sounded as if "all the percussion instrument players in a large orchestra had suddenly gone berserk."

Since every object has its own keynote, naturally there is concord between some and discord between others. This often accounts for the incompatibility of certain individuals and for the preference that everyone has for certain seasons, places, colors, and music. Where keynotes harmonize there is pleasurable association; where they do not, the sensibilities are jarred. Then we say quite rightly that this or that "gets on our nerves."

Not knowing the cause for the dissonant condition and circumstances in which we may find ourselves, we go on struggling with the handicap, often quite needlessly. Here again "knowledge becomes the wings whereon we fly to heaven."

When humanity shall have developed clairaudience together with the ability to determine the keynote of any person or thing, then friends, places and poisitons will be selected in accordance with basic tonal compatibility.

Every musical genius, for instance, realizes his greatest achievements in composition in the key which governs his life. Again, a conductor can best interpret the works of the composer whose compositions are concordant with his own keynote. Where there is perfect inner rapport between the composer, the interpreter, and the thing interpreted, naturally there is the sympathetic understanding which makes for exceptional skill in rendition.

Let us consider further the inner significance of the number five and the important part it plays in esoteric musical interpretation. The chord is formed by the first, third, and fifth notes of the scale. These three tones represent musically the powers of the Trinity, namely, the Father, Son and Holy Ghost, or the Will, Wisdom, and Activity principles as embodied in human expression. The first tone represents the Will or Power aspect by which all things are brought into being. The second tone represents the Love-Wisdom aspect of the Christ by which all things are interpreted into a unified whole. The third tone represents the Activity principle which works either constructively or destructively, in the one instance building for health, harmony and plenty, in the other manifesting disease, limitation and lack.

Frequent repetition of the chord of one's own keynote produces a soothing, harmonious effect on strained nerves or a tired body. The playing of this chord is a splendid way in which to lift the consciousness above the vicissitudes of personal living and into the realms of inner knowing where all is permanent harmony, peace and love.

The utterance of musical harmonies depends upon the tonal concord of the planets making them. As previously stated, the twelve semitones of the octave are a perfect replica of the twelve-powered cosmic scheme. The five zodiacal Hierarchies that have passed beyond the environs of our solar system are as follows:

ARIES—Keynote D-flat major, which has five flats: B, E, A, D and G.
TAURUS—Keynote E-flat major, which has three flats: B, E and A.
GEMINI—Keynote F-sharp major, which has six sharps: F, C, G, D, A and E.
CANCER—Keynote G-sharp major, which has six sharps: C, G, D, A, E and B, and F doublesharp.
 (The signature used by musicians is A-flat major, which has four flats, B, E, A, and D.)
LEO—Keynote A-sharp major, which has four sharps; D, A, E and B, and three double sharps, F, C and G.
 (The signature used by musicians is B-flat major, which has two flats, namely, B and E.)

The following Hierarchies are still actively engaged in forwarding our planetary evolution:

VIRGO—Keynote C-major, which has no sharps or flats.
LIBRA—Keynote D-major, which has two sharps: F and C.
SCORPIO—Keynote E-major, which has four sharps: F, C, G and D.
SAGITTARIUS—Keynote F-major, which has one flat: B.
CAPRICORN—Keynote G-major, has one sharp: F.
AQUARIUS—Keynote A-major, has three sharps: F, C and G.
PISCES—Keynote B-major, has five sharps: F, C, G, D and A.

Each of the twelve signs exercises rulership over a certain center in the human body, wherein its forces are focussed and its influence is particularly effective. Every organ of the body is formed of an aggregate of countless minute atoms, all of which are in continuous motion. Thus every organ in the body bears the asterial signature or the impress of the zodiacal sign governing it. Since the keynotes of both are identical, an organ is particularly amenable to the vibratory rhythm of the sign that rules it.

Everything on earth is a manifestation of the four principles, Fire, Air, Water and Earth. This "Immortal Four" constitutes the Magic Word by which everything was made that is made. These mighty emanations are rayed upon the earth through the tones of the twelve zodiacal Hierarchies which are stepped down to man as the twelve notes of the chromatic scale.

The cosmic chord is also composed of three notes, namely, first, third, and fifth of the octave. The number one is God; the number three is His threefold power, namely, Will, Wisdom, and Activity, or the attributes of the Father, the Son, and the Holy Ghost, respectively. The number five is man in whom these qualities are to be evolved, since the purpose of earth life is to furnish the disciplines by which man may become, ultimately, even as the gods.

On the first Creative Day, the celestial beings of Leo, through the tone of A-sharp major, fashioned the matrix of man's physical body with its germinal sense organs and awakened the slumbering divinity within.

The chord that played upon the earth on the first Creative Day was sounded by Aries (1), Gemini (3), and Leo (5), thus conforming to the one, three and five that make up the musical chord. Aries through the scale of D-flat major (which is also C-sharp) gave the first impulse of life; Gemini through the scale of F-sharp major set into motion the masculine and feminine polaities, or the positive and negative forces in nature. Leo through the scale of A-sharp major formed the divine pattern of the potential god-man.

Similarly, each of the seven Creative Days strikes its own individual keynote through the cosmic chords of its gleaming zodiacal Arbiters.

The cosmic minor chords work correspondingly during the assimilative periods of the cosmic nights when the earth and all that it contains are reunited in the arms of Infinity (Chaos), and when every unit of life both gives to and receives from every other unit the essence of its accumulated experiences. This process of universal interchange is effected by means of the intoning harmonies of the cosmic minor chords. Thus heaven and earth and all that lives therein, are built in harmony with the music of the spheres.

The cosmic matrix in which exists the divine pattern for the evolution of the entire human race is fashioned by the music of the twelve celestial Hierarchies. In a corresponding manner the matrix or divine image upon which an incoming Ego is to build its body is also attuned to the harmonies of the stellar chords during the prenatal period when the embryo takes form. This image, or archetype, is a vortex of creative color and sound, and is attuned in the heaven world to the keynote of the Ego that is to inhabit it.

Each of the seven planets sounds its own keynote, which is identical with one of the seven tones of the musical scale. Each Ego vibrates in harmony with one of the seven planets. The notes of all the planets are necessary to build the archetype of the Ego, but each planetary tone is adapted to harmonize with the particular planet which sounds the soul-key of the individual. This note is centered in the medulla oblongata, the large nerve center located in the back of the head, and may be distinctly heard by anyone possessing the gift of clairaudience.

The sevenfold body of man vibrates primarily to this same key in ascending rhythms. When the work assigned to one octave is finished, that of the next higher octave is taken up, with each succeeding scale vibrating at twice the rate of the one preceding it. Thus humanity intones in miniature the music of the spheres.

MUSIC AND THE PRENATAL LIFE

> *What is the human body but a constellation of the same powers that formed the stars in the sky.*
> —Paracelsus.

The incoming ego during its prenatal journey is particularly susceptible to the influence of the twelve supreme Lords of Light, the zodiacal Hierarchies. During the first three months of this journey the spirit coming into physical birth is cared for and protected by hosts of angels.

When prospective mothers come to know and realize the great building and sustaining powers of music in the formation of body and character during these sacred motnhs of preparation, they will bathe the soul daily in music attuned to the keys of D-flat major (Aries), E-flat major (Taurus), and F-sharp major (Gemini), respectively.

With the fourth month the Ego comes nearer to the vibrations of earth and the incoming life tunes in more closely to the physical world. At this time the keynote of G-sharp major (Cancer), exercises a dominant influence.

During the fifth and sixth months, the Love and Wisdom principles of Leo and Virgo, respectively, are interwoven into the fabric of the soul to the keynotes of A-sharp major and C-natural major.

The seventh month is a crucial period for the incarnating spirit; it involves a microcosmic contest for supremacy between spirit and form. Libran composiitons in D-major are musical aids of special value at this testing time.

With the eighth month the Ego passes under the impress of mortality. The song of Scorpio in E-major proclaims that the body need not bear the signature of death, but that it can become attuned with life eternal.

The music in the key of F-major (Sagittarius) ushers in the ninth or birth month.

After the spirit is born into this outer, physical world, the first three months come under the rulership of the last three zodiacal signs, namely, Capricorn, Aquarius, and Pisces, each governing a month in the order named.

Thus, we see that the newborn babe remains in close contact with its celestial guardians. In Wordsworth's words: "Heaven lies about us in our infancy." Many are the eyes that can bear witness to the tender and loving angelic ministrations during this period.

Thrice blessed are the "little wanderers from heaven," who during the first three months of their life among mortals can be surrounded with music in the keys of G-major, A-major, and B-major, the keynotes of their celestial guardians during this period.

MUSIC OF THE ZODIAC IN RELATION TO THE HUMAN BODY

The body of man is his home, the architect who builds it is the astral world. The carpenters are at one time Jupiter, at another Mars, at one time Taurus and at another Orion. Man is a sun and moon and a heaven filled with stars.
— Paracelsus.

Studied carefully in relation to the stars, the entire human body will be found to re-echo the music of the spheres.

Aries through the key of D-flat major awakens the divine impulses of life and fashions a perfect image of the head, the intricacies of ear and eye and all the ramifications of the cranial nerves as these are organized to function harmoniously with spiritual being.

Taurus through the key of A-flat major projects the first form patterns within which the spirit functions in time and space. The Taurian emanation bears the spiritual impress of the throat and the larnyx, organs which are destined to become the foremost seat of power in the human body.

Gemini through the key of F-sharp major unites life with form enabling the spirit to become indwelling within the body. Gemini gives the pattern of dual bodily impulses and bears the perfected image of the arms and the vital breath center, the lungs.

Cancer through G-sharp major awakens the faculty of intuition, and for the physical body bears the impress of the stomach.

The Hierarchy of Leo, the brilliant Lords of Flame, working through A-sharp major radiate from their own bodies of light, the nucleus upon which man builds his physical body. This spark of life is centered in the heart and it is the love-force by means of which the body will ultimately attain perfection.

Virgo contains the archetype of the intestines and all the intricate workings connected therewith. Operating through C-natural, this sign also awakens in man the divine wisdom of the soul.

Libra gives the pattern of the purifcatory organs, the kidneys, and through D-major awakens the faculty of discrimination.

Scorpio bears the archetypal image of the organs of generation which are the bearers of the mystery of creation. This sign, working through E-major, sounds the note of purity and regeneration, the ultimate state toward which humanity is aspiring.

Sagittarius holds the pattern of the higher mind and its spiritual mystery. This is its supreme gift to man and through F-major its service is to awaken spiritual power and nourish the aspiration which will give the higher mind supremacy over the lower material mind.

Capricorn holds the pattern of the knees. Here are certain sensitive points or inner centers of power which are destined for future unfoldment. This sign, using the key of G-major, sheds a renewing ray of divine effulgence upon the earth, hence the important work of this Hierarchy upon the desire body of humanity.

Aquarius (A-major) contains the archetypal image of the ankles. This sign is also aiding the development of the etheric vehicle. When the extended senses of this body are fully developed, disease and death will be no more and God (good) shall wipe away all tears, for the old shall have passed and made way for the new.

Pisces (B-major) contains the perfected image of the feet, the foundation of understanding. When these shall have come to function properly, man "shall walk and not be weary; he shall run and not faint." The Piscean Hierarchy also works with the entire physical body. Unity is the keynote of Pisces, and as the race learns under this sign to unify all life, it will enter into a full realization of what is signified by the statement, "Made in the image and likeness of God."

HEALING AND MUSIC

"Music is Life and Life is Music"

The healing values of music have been recognized from the earliest times. Paracelsus, the most illustrious of all therapeutic seers, drew upon the powers of this art in his ministry for the cure of varied ills, mental, moral and physical. Special compositions were prescribed for certain maladies in accordance with vibratory law. He literally practiced what he termed a "musical medicine."

That the art of musical healing is now being rapidly restored to us is evident from many quarters. Substantial contributions are being made to this end by the scientist, the medical practitioner, and the psychologist, as well as by the interpretrers of music itself.

Since the universe and all its parts, including the body of man, is built through the power of rhythmic vibration, it follows that a scientific application of musical rhythm can be advantageously utilized for both the restoration and the maintenance of physical well being. Radiant and perfect health exists when there is complete harmony between the keynote of the etheric vehicle, which is the vitalizing principle of the physical body, and the keynote of the archetype, the heavenly pattern in the likeness of which the physical body is moulded.

All discordant emotions, negative thinking, and destructive passions, such as anger, hatred, lust, and particularly fear, introduce discord into the vital and physical bodies and generally lower their tone and interfere with their normal functions. This introduces a dissonance between the keynotes of the two vehicles which in turn reacts upon the physical body as lack of ease, or dis-ease. "As a man thinketh in his heart, so is he," is a statement embodying a more far-reaching truth than is generally recognized even by metaphysicians. This statement is, moreover, a powerful healing affirmation.

As man comes to learn the musical laws underlying the creation and operation of the universe, or macrocosm, and the application of these same musical principles to the sustenance and well being of his own body, the microcosm, he comes to realize more fully the truth of the Master's statement: "Verily thou art the temple of the living God."

At the conclusion of the World War in 1918, some intensely interesting experiments along the line of musico-therapy were conducted by Margaret Anderton, a musician and nurse, among wounded Canadian soldiers. Her findings are so completely in harmony with the teachings of occultism on this subject that we herewith quote from a published interview given by Miss Anderton to the press at the time.

"There are two chief ways of treating patients," said Miss Anderton, "though in detail no two cases can be treated alike. But, as a general thing, I administer the music for any form of war-neurosis, which is largely mental, and have the man produce the music himself in orthopedic cases or those of paralysis. Different instruments are used for different types of trouble. The timbre of an instrument probably plays the largest part in musical healing, and for this reason wind instruments are good because of their peculiar quality. Wood instruments are particularly potent for a certain kind of war-neurosis because of their penetrating, sustained tone. Instruments are usually better than vocal music, for with the human voice the personal element, which is usually not desirable, enters in. At times, however, the voice is the best. The timbre of wood instruments, however, affects the nerve centers more than does the voice or the piano. This timbre is especially good with deaf people, who feel the vibrations in the spine.

"Some of the cures seem little short of miraculous—and it depends on the definition of the word miracle whether they are short of it. Memories have been brought back to men suffering with amnesia; acute temporary insanity done away with; paralyzed muscles restored. One captain who had been hurled into the air and then buried in debris at the bursting of a bomb had never been able to remember even his own name until the music restored him."

Musico-therapy may be harmful as well as beneficial. Mere playing for soldiers is not musico-therapy and may often be very detrimental to wounded, convalescent, or mentally depressed cases if done without knowledge of the needs of the men or the basic laws underlying music and the technique of using it for purposes of healing. Nor is knowledge of music alone sufficient. There is need also of the application of the sciences of physics and psychology, and of the anatomy of the human body, espeically the structure and mechanism of the nervous and muscular systems.

The report of Miss Anderton's work continues:

"Tests have been made upon healthy men, and it has been ascertained that certain pitches or harmonic combinations have a certain bodily effect. At present the effect on the throat of a certain chord in a certain key is being investigated, and it may prove to be of help in dealing with paralysis of the jaw.

"The correspondence between color and sound vibrations is also threaded into the healing work. This, too, has been worked on for years by Miss Anderton. 'I had often thought about it,' she said, 'but it was crystallized for me one night after a concert when a man came to me in a state of great excitement and asked me why he had seen a certain color around the piano all the time that I was playing a certain composition. I looked up the vibrations of the dominant tone of the piece'."

Experiments have been tried with the human voice at the New York State Hospital for the Insane on Ward's Island. Physicians said it was shown that tired nerves and brain were soothed by song and that vocal music was more effective in treating the insane than was instrumental music. Among other observations recorded from these experiments were the following: The soprano voice was most beneficial in cases of acute malancholia; the tenor voice, high and clear, had the best effect on persons having softening of the brain, while the deep, rich tones of the baritone best served the paranoiacs.

It has been well demonstrated again and again that an unbalanced mind is particularly sensitive to musical vibrations. A professional pianist in Russia, trying solos on mental patients, found that jazz was positively harmful, while soft, soothing, restful music would quiet the most violent. Making practical use of this knowledge to national and racial ends, the Soviets some years ago were reported to have prohibited the sale of phonograph jazz records.

The Los Angeles County General Hospital has also done some experimental healing work with music. Treatments have been conducted under the supervision of the Chaplain of the Institution, together with the heads of the tubercular and psychopathic departments.

Another pioneer in musico-therapy is Harriet Ayers Seymour, chairman of the Music Division of the Hospital Visiting Committee of New York. Her experience has been carried on with the cooperation of doctors in various hospitals for many years.

Here is a partial list of some of her musical prescriptions:

> Of benefit to persons suffering from paralysis and disorders of the joints: Sousa's marches, The Anvil Chorus, William Tell Overture, Brahms' Hungarian Dances, By the Waters of the Minnetonka.
> Of benefit to persons afflicted with tuberculosis: Strauss' waltzes, La Paloma, Minuet in G, Schubert's Serenade, March of the Wooden Soldiers, Brahms' Lullaby, Schubert's Ave Maria, From the Land of the Sky Blue Water, Somewhere, Over the Rainbow.
> Beneficial to persons being otherwise treated for heart trouble: The Barcarolle, The Blue Danube, Chopin's A-Minor Waltz, Tango music, Humoresque, Cui's Orientale, Song of India, Donna e Mobile, Oley Speake's Sylvia.
> For persons suffering from insomnia and from pain generally: Mendelssohn's Spring Song, Meditation from Thais, Chopin's Preludes, On Wings of Song, *Andante*, Beethoven's Fifth Symphony, *Adagio*, Beethoven's Pathetique Symphony.
> For soothing persons suffering from certain mental and nervous afflictions: Rhythmic folk songs, County Derry, songs of Stephen Foster, Spanish tangoes, Brahms' Hungarian dances, Sousa's marches, Strauss' Waltzes, Gilbert and Sullivan, Indian Love Call, My Wild Irish Rose, Wishing, Estrellita.

Miss Seymour has pointed out that in order to derive the most benefit from use of music as supplementary environmental treatment of various persons, each individual case must be taken into consideration. For example, "Meditation from Thais" might benefit one person in grave pain, but might irritate another.

The following excerpt from a United Press dispatch, October 17th, 1941, carrying the Chicago dateline, records yet another experiment leading toward a future adoption of music as a universal healing agent. The item follows:

> Soft strains of classical music which she alone could hear today obscured travail of childbirth for a mother whose first child was delivered by Caesarean section.
> Dr. Edward L. Cornell, who performed the operation, approved the experiment by which radio music was carried to the patient through special ear plugs. "It is a progressive step," he asserted. "We have more work to do, but it obviously caused a satisfactory distraction."
> The mother thought th musical accompaniment "just wonderful." She heard "Tales from the Vienna Woods," parts of the "Fortune Teller," and "L'Amour, Toujours L'Amour" before Tschaikowsky's concerto in B-flat minor was put on at the climax of the delivery. The patient had only a local anesthetic.
> The experiment was supervised by Cornell with the assistance of Dr. Leonarde Keeler, who regulated the flow of music.
> The mother selected the music herself. It was played by a frequency modulation radio station, eliminating pauses for announcements.
> Previous operations, including childbirth, have been accompanied by music, but not in such manner as today—where no one in the room but the mother and Keeler, with auxiliary earphones, could hear the sounds. In other experiments, physicians had found music distracting to them thus endangering their patients.
> Keeler said the vast range of music materially improved the experiment, capturing the listener's attention more than common radio tones do. He said further experiments will be

made, but he predicted that the method probably would gain widespread use in hospitals.

It is particularly interesting to note that the young mother selected Tschaikowsky's Concerto in B-flat minor as the composition with which the incoming Ego was to be welcomed into its new mundane experience. The soul signature of this Ego is probably more subjective than objective, thus leading the mother through her love for the incoming spirit to choose music set in a minor key.

MUSIC AS A HEALING AGENT FOR INSANITY

When music as a healing agent becomes more generally recognized, it will perhaps be utilized more extensively in the earlier stage of mental cases than with any other. It is quite naturally felt that such patients can be reached more immediately and effectively than patients afflicted with physical ailments. Man's threefold body is linked to the threefold spirit by means of the mind. As previously stated, each of these vehicles or principles sound a keynote of its own. If these notes be altered so as to create a dissonance between the bodies great enough to cause a rupture between any two of them, the result is some form of mental derangement.

In idiocy it is the harmonious connection between the etheric and desire bodies that is disturbed. The etheric body is under Aquarius and is keyed to A-major, 3 sharps; the desire body is under Capricorn, keyed to G-major, 1 sharp. The mind is under Sagittarius, F-major, 1 flat. The spirit is under Leo and keyed to B-flat major, 2 flats.

When a break occurs between the desire body and the mind the result is a raving maniac. A break between the mind and the spirit has the effect of rendering the victim virtually devoid of conscience. It produces the clever, cunning mind, the soulless person capable of committing the most unspeakable crimes.

Music in the related keys will prove beneficial in the treatment of these various forms of mental aberration. From the type of insanity may be diagnosed the nature of the mental break after which the case can be beneficially treated by music in the keys corresponding to the afflicted vehicles. The keynote of the threefold body of humanity at large is B-major, and is correlated to Pisces. The note of the spirit, as previously observed, is A-sharp major (Leo).

As we have already observed, the body of man is keyed to the entire range of the chromatic scale. With disease comes a dissonance between the tones. This is particularly noticeable in insanity.

The atmosphere surrounding a hospital for the insane is permeated with the dissonances of broken notes. A sensitive is acutely conscious of this fact and of its debilitating effect upon highly sensitized patients. Naturally this retards the recovery of such inmates. Here is to be found one important reason for the slow response to treatment in many cases. Scientific application of musico-therapy can do much to remedy this condition.

As already observed, F is the keynote of the earth. It is also the notes of the mental signs Gemini and Sagittarius (F-sharp and F-natural, respecitvely). This fact points to the prime purpose of man's evolution on earth which is the development of the power of mind. The attainment of universal intelligence and the identification with divine mind is his goal.

When the vibrational activity of a certain organ departs from its normal condition and the accustomed rhythm is broken, disease results. The mind, being a creative instrument and the channel through which the powers of the spirit work upon the body, is capable of becoming the principal agent in any form of healing. Since this is so, musical treatment should in all cases be directed first of all to quieting the mind, establishing it in harmony, and then quickening its powers for the work it is called upon to do in the healing of any physical ailment. This can best be accomplished by playing chords in the scale of F and F-sharp.

A body ailment is not always indicated in the horoscope by the sign governing the part afflicted. Sometimes it is denoted by the opposite sign, since the forces of the opposites intermingle in the body. For example, Taurus and Scorpio are opposing signs, the first ruling the throat, the latter the organs of generation. Consequently throat trouble may come from afflictions in either Taurus or Scorpio. That it comes from Scorpio in many cases is particularly evident in adolescents. At the age of puberty when the forces of Scorpio are especially active, the reaction of the throat is decidedly marked, one way or another. In boys it makes for a change in voice. Sometimes the nature of the configuration is such that the throat ailment passes with adolescence; at other times the trouble is accentuated.

The close relationship existing between opposite signs appears musically in their respective keynotes. For instance, in the two signs above considered, Taurus and Scorpio, the former sounds the note of E-flat and the latter E-natural.

Music in the key of E carries the quality of purity and healing through regeneration, E-flat being more effective for Egos in feminine bodies and E-sharp for those in masculine form. In view of these facts it is well to select music in the key of E for children passing through their second septenary, when the desire body unfolds its power from latency into dynamic expression.

Healing will be permanent only when based on and in accord with man's spiritual nature and constitution. Throat ailments, for instance, will pass with man's regeneration. And not only this, but the throat will then become the center of the creative force which now functions at the base of the spine. Its functions will have been lifted to a higher level. The spoken word will then carry the power of direct creation. Thus it was that God created heaven and earth, and all therein. Man, made in His image, will some day do no less.

Gemini governs the lungs and also the forces of the human mind as distinguished from the higher or divine mind. Inharmony of bodily rhythm will ultimately externalize itself in the physical body. Tuberculosis, for example, may be traced to pronounced materialistic thinking in lives past. Sagittarius, the opposite sign of Gemini, governs the base of the spine and the sacral bones. It is in this portion of the body that the spiritual fires are first lighted to burn away the dross of the lower nature and extract therefrom that pure essence which becomes the living waters of eternal life referred to by Jesus. Sagittarius also governs the awakened or Christed mind, a state following mental purification and the redemption of the body. To repeat, Gemini sounds the keynote of F-sharp and Sagittarius, F-natural. The office of the key of F is to open up the avenues for the forces of mental purification and regeneration just as the powers of E work for the cleansing and redemption of the physical body.

Another pair of opposites are Cancer and Capricorn, the former ruling the stomach, the latter the knees. Afflications of the stomach result from unbridled appetites in the past and diseases of the limbs from unrighteous living. Spiritually, Capricorn elevates man to the place where the Christ consciousness is born within him and Cancer promotes him to the transcendant glories of Initiation. The keynote of Cancer is G-sharp and that of Capricorn is G-natural. The key of G releases the forces of spiritual illumination. The initial pitch is sounded in the simple or natural key; the subjective qualities released by the sign are contacted in man by the flats and the objective qualities are released and contacted in a similar way through the sharps.

Aries governs the head with its various organs, and Libra, its opposite sign, the kidneys. Spiritually interpreted, Aries releases the highest impulses of the spirit and Libra builds the wisdom that is of the soul. The keynote of Aries is D-flat and that of Libra is D-natural. D is therefore a harmonic incantation which releases a renewal of spiritual force for man's restoration when afflictions center in the organs governed by these signs.

Virgo governs the intestines, and its opposite sign, Pisces, the feet. The keynote of Virgo is service through chastity and that of Pisces is service through unity. The keynote of Virgo is C-major; Pisces, B-major. The musical impulses of Virgo-Pisces manifest through the tones of B and C and sound a call to service. Healing for afflictions of these two signs is most easily effected in their fundamental spiritual features through service rendered to others. These ailments are seldom of such a nature as to prevent service of some kind, though a special effort of the will is sometimes necessary for accomplishment. The vibrations of the note B will also aid in developing the power of the will.

Leo governs the heart, and its opposite polarity, Aquarius, the ankles. The keynote of Leo is A-sharp; Aquarius, A-natural. The motive power of Leo is love; of Aquarius, mentality. Their combination on the highest plane of manifestation will produce the superman of the coming Aquarian Age. To achieve this union of heart and mind is a difficult process and usually involves adjustments not possible without suffering temporary inharmonies.

The keynote of A breathes forth a radiant force which man can translate at its highest into true humility and compassion. When this quality of Leo and Aquarius becomes dominant in the life of man the ills which now afflict the personal life, both mental and physical, will pass away. This is the supreme truth conveyed in the musical message of A.

KEYNOTES OF MASTER MUSICIANS

A few years ago *The Beacon* published a treatise entitled *Music, Physician of the Etheric Man*. This article opened such fascinating and illuminating vistas for further esoteric research in connection with the work of the three greatest immortals of the musical world, that we quote from it at length. These three masters, Beethoven, Bach, and Wagner, all came to provide musical channels through the ethers by which the healing powers of tone might reach man's etheric or vitalizing principle, the health and harmony of which must first be established before a like reaction is possible in the physical body. We quote herewith excerpts from the above mentioned article:

> Bach was a Mercurian and the healing vibration of his music is etheric; but etheric music alone cannot answer man's need, so Bach, of Mercury-Venus, retired . . . preparing the way for the great Martian, Beethoven. Unlike Bach, the scores of Beethoven reach into the material body of mankind, and stir its substances into life anew. Each of his nine mighty symphonies is designed to stimulate the etheric and physical centers of the human family. It is to be noted that Beethoven, healing from the etheric point of view, accomplished again, not completion, but preparation for the tenth way. In each great musical triumph, Beethoven, the Martian, descended to the human consciousness, and then in turn and in sequence stimulated each of the centers through which it had succeeded in bringing his own inspiration perfectly, mounting through each center to the highest plane of Reality he, himself, had achieved from the Earth plane.
>
> The Martian could align with the Spirit of the New Age, and voice all of the past with Venusian understanding and with Martian strength—but he could not align the very spirit with all Cosmos in himself and voice it in his work. Yet,

born in the sounds of Beethoven's immortal symphonies is all of the higher planetary healing present in Sun, Mercury, Venus, Earth, Mars, Jupiter, Saturn, and Neptune.

Any student of the higher celestial sciences can readily determine the types of healing thus brought for universal well-being. An attuned sensitized Master may readily determind which passages might be prescribed to rememdy human ills, for it is characteristic of the Master that each center, physical, and etheric, should have its place, and each be in its place, musically, scientifically, and mystically interpreted.

Uranus, soul awakener and healer, came in Wagner not only to awaken, but to sweep man, body, soul, and spirit into the Cosmic Consciousness . . . stimulating etheric, physical, and soul centers alike.

Wagner's themes are taken from the etheric by a conscious Master, set to the sounds and colors adapted to the healing of three planes simultaneously, and, with the cooperation and physical assistance of the Earth Master, are keyed to permit the physical man to enter into the spirit which has forever rested in close attunement with the Real.

Bach, Beethoven, and Wagner are forerunners of the divine music of the future. This will, in sound, color, and fragrance, heal instantly any disharmony in man, for man will be attuned to his own systemic rhythms, and perfectly radiate and reflect Cosmic Reality, man's prototype.

REGENERATION THROUGH MUSIC

Music is an art imbued with power to penetrate into the very depth of the soul, imbuing man with the love of virtue.
—Plato

Music constitutes an integral part of the moral content of man's character. The moral force of music rests on the correspondences existing between its tonal patterns and those of the ideal world. It sounds forth a superior order, it enunciates man's highest law.

Pythagoras held that man's nature experienced a purification when hearing solemn songs sung to the accompaniment of a lyre.

The influence of music as a cure for crime has been used with marked effectiveness in France. So successful has been the response of hitherto incorrigible children to the influence of high and lofty music that concert artists were engaged to give regularly scheduled performances in the reform schools in and around Paris.

The healing and building qualities of music were utilized extensively in the early Mysteries. Chants, mantrams, and invocations used in the Temple services were musically constructed in the light of spiritual science and were, therefore, deeply occult and productive of important spiritual results.

The keynotes of the seven planetary spirits before the throne of God were intoned in the sacred temples of Egypt. In Greece the seven vowels of the Grecian language were used as a channel for the inpouring of these planetary sounds that worked so powerfully in their regenerative effect upon the Temple neophytes.

Since every human being is keyed to one of the planets, it was possible for the Temple Priest in the ancient Mystery Schools to determine the keynote of a pupil and to teach him how to attune himself to the planet of a like note, his parent star, and thereby draw on spiritual power of transcendent degree. This wisdom was part of the Mysteries, the light of which, having been allowed to go out, leaves our priesthood lacking much of this deeper wisdom possessed by the Templars of ancient days.

The Persians celebrated the entry of the sun into each zodiacal sign with appropriate music stressing the vibratory keynote of the presiding Hierarchy at the time. The more advanced celebrants were able to place themselves in harmony with the music of their own particular sign and planet and receive benefits accordingly.

At certain times in the course of history a "magical music" has been brought to earth by some high Initiate. The beautiful legends of Greece tell of Orpheus as being such a musical messenger and that by his rare skill troubled minds were stilled, flowers bloomed, waters became calm, and winds ceased. The Old Testament carries this same truth in the story of David, the sweet and illumined singer of Israel, who by the power of his magic harp soothed the madness of Saul.

The most profound truths connected with the teachings concealed in that supreme and sacred ceremonial, The Last Supper, as was performed by the Lord Chirst, are based upon the use of vibratory power. These truths He imparted at that time to His Chosen Twelve.

The rhythms of certain high and noble music raise the pitch and accelerate the motion of every atom in the body; they also activate dynamically certain vital centers hitherto latent and work, moreover, upon the mind, tending to lift it from its confinement in the concrete to freedom in the abstract.

There are seven centers, or "musical lights," to be awakened in man's body. These centers lie along the spinal cord and correspond with the seven notes of the octave. They are not physical, but etheric, and serve as conductors of specialized vital essences to the physical centers. These centers receive this force through corresponding etheric plexes which not only contact the physical centers, but interprenetrate them completely.

The first of these vital points is situated at the base of the spine; its color is red. Here the serpentine Kundalini sleeps. When this slumbering fire first awakens, its dark color begins to lighten in hue, and as the regenerative process continues through the gradual rising of the spinal spirit fire it becomes a pure, luminous, ruby red. The stimulation of this center produces the beginnings of psychic abilities.

The next, or second center, is the solar plexus, also called the epigastric plexus. Its corresponding etheric center is known as "the sun of the stomach." Its color is reddish orange. As the work of transmutation goes on, those colors are modified by radiations of a soft green light. With the awakening of this center comes the first trace of clairvoyance.

The third, or hypogastric plexus, is correlated to the spleen. When this becomes active it radiates with all the golden splendor of a miniature sun. This center, when awakened, bestows the gift of healing. In the early stages of its development there is a blend of green light with gold, which later takes on the effulgence of pure gold.

The fourth, or cardiac plexus, is over the heart. This is a vital point of peculiar sensitiveness and emits a luminous, soft, yellow radiance which in the higher stages of transmuattion becomes tinged with ethereal blue. The development of this center brings memories of past life cycles. This is the power referred to in occult parlance as "heart memory."

The fifth center is the pharyngeal plexus located in the throat just over the larynx. Its color is azure blue and the refining processes of the body cause it to sparkle and glow with silver lights. The development of this center brings a recovery of the Lost Word. The creative power of speech is its high function. "My words shall accomplish that whereunto they are sent," proclaimed the Master of Masters who possessed the power belonging to this center.

The sixth, or cavernous plexus, is situated in the head at a point between the eyebrows. When fully developed there ray forth from this point kaleidoscopic color patterns of indescribable beauty of splendor, their primary tones being rose, yellow, blue and purple. When this center functions fully, consciousness is continuous, neither sleep nor death interrupting it henceforth. The seventh, or chorioid plexus, is in the top of the head. When the body has been fully regenerated this center emits a pure white effulgent light, blessing all who come under its luminous, healing rays. Its development brings liberation from the wheel of birth and death. "He that overcometh, I will make a pillar in the Temple of my God, and he shall go out thence no more," is a statement referring to One who has attained to this high state.

Thus we see that the several etheric centers in the vital body unfold their powers progressively from the lowest to the highest as regeneration takes place, and that the seven-toned musical scale to which these centers correspond sound forth their respective notes in accordance with man's development. The lifting of the spinal spirit fire is in perfect accompaniment to the tones of the musical scale. The expanding consciousness releases one note after another in an ever ascending series. In this way the body of man becomes more and more closely attuned to that larger body known as the Grand Man of the Universe, both sounding forth the music of the spheres. Rudolph Steiner, the eminent Rosicrucian occultist, refers to this development as "the wonder of the octave experience." Dr. George S. Arundale, Theosophical writer and teacher, describes this same scientific truth with a poet's imagination when he declares: "The Kundalini is music as it is color. It is a rainbow as it is a perfect song."

The single string of the monochord has its counterpart in the spinal cord of man, the lower part of which is connected with the generative organs (earth) and the upper part with the head (heaven).

On the monochord, the interval between heaven and earth is conceived as being spanned by the double octave. Similarly, when man has harmoniously developed the double octave of the physical and the etheric, he, too, will have an instrument that will make him a conscious citizen even here and now of two worlds. To sound the upper or heavenly notes of the monochord is to know liberation from the cycle of recurrent birth. To sound the lower note is to establish an understanding accord with humanity at large that has not yet risen above the deadening toils of transitory physical existence. To sound the two is "To walk with kings (Master-Initiates), nor lose the common touch."

The diapason of struggle for supremacy is sounding continuously upon the human monochord between the Luciferian spirits on the one hand and the angels on the other. Therefore, as the Lucifers are endeavoring to keep this channel charged with the fiery forces of Mars, the angels strive to suffuse it with ethereal lunar radiations.

As regeneration supersedes generation in the life of the individual, the spirit fire in the spinal column, the human monochord, is awakened, and the tonal pitch is gradually raised as the sacred creative fire ascends toward the head. By this process the natural man is at length transformed into the celestial man.

In the cosmic monochord, the earth, the sun, and the heavens all sound the same identical note, the difference being one of octave only. Man, a creature innately divine, is being worked upon by Neptune, the planet of divinity, in a manner calculated to arouse and lift the inner, sacred fires of his being so that the key of his soul will harmonize with the heavenly chord instead of that of the earth.

The call of man, in the words of one of the greatest of all biblical seers, is to "Put off the old man and put on the new."

It was the ecstatic realization of this unity with the divine selfhood within, that brought forth from that illumined medieval seer, Angelus Silesius, his victorious chant:

> *In all eternity there is no tone so sweet*
> *As when man's heart with God's doth beat.*

Rudolph Steiner states that when man can steep himself sufficiently in the consciousness of the Saturn Period he will know again the lost secret of architecture; when he can enter into the direct consciousness of the Sun Period he will know the full mystery of sculpture; and that with the full consciousness of the Moon Period he will enter into the mystery of painting. To the present Earth Period belongs the mystery of music, the last of the arts to be developed, as it is the highest of them all. During what may be spoken of as the "Cathedral Age" in Europe, master workmen were in incarnation whose labors indicated that they were qualified to receive the wages permitting them "to travel in foreign countries." The Greeks of the Golden Age of Pericles were masters of the art of sculpture. The 15th and 16th centuries produced the masters of color and also the towering geniuses of the literature and drama of the Elizabethan Era. Music, of all the arts, remains yet in its infancy.

The first real school of music is said to have been founded by the prophet Samuel among the Levite choristers, with David as its music master and the Psalms as its hymnal. These Psalms are an Initiate's musically poetic description of the awakening of the seven centers previously mentioned and the successive steps in their unfoldment.

The seven-stringed harp of David was within himself. It was by means of his own spiritually awakened powers that he soothed the madness of Saul. It was by the magic of this same seven-stringed harp that David built for himself that spiritual armor that protected him from Saul at the time when Saul would have taken David's life. This celestial harp is also the seven-stringed lyre of Orpheus with which he calmed the waters and caused the tempest to cease.

Consider further the nature of this seven-stringed harp as it exists within the body of man. There are seven cavities or ventricles within the brain, each sounding its own note and emanating its own individual color. This sevenfold tone is a miniature choral of the celestial song intoned by the seven Planetary Spirits before the throne of God, namely, Uranus, Saturn, Jupiter, Mars, Earth, Venus and Mercury.

The brain cavities are filled with a subtile life essence, now dormant in most people, but which begin to glow or sparkle with inconceivable brilliance as man develops his spiritual nature. Physiologically, these seven centers bear the following names: Olfactory, Lateral, Third, Fourth, the Cavernous Ventricles, and the Pineal and Pituitary Glands.

The lyre, or the harp of seven strings, has always borne much esoteric symbolism. Hargrave Jennings in *The Rites and Mysteries of the Rosicrucians* thus describes it:

> The seven strings of the magic harp sound the music of the spheres. They mean also the seven tones of pure music and stand again for the seven prismatic colors which again describe the seven vowels by which speech first came to man. They represent also the seven rulers of the seven planets which have their seven spirits or Celestial Flames which are the seven angels or Spirits of God who keep the way round about the Throne of the Ancient of Days.

Music in its highest spiritual aspects is on the way toward a recovery of much that has been lost, and also to a further development of this, the youngest and the highest of all the arts. As this phase devleops, music will become an increasingly important factor in the work of groups devoted to healing by the power of the spoken word, and to the work involved in the attainment of spiritual illumination.

The Grail music of Richard Wagner is literally a transcription of the music of angelic choirs and was given to earth for the specific purpose of furthering man's spiritual evolution. It possesses the highest vibratory rate of any music yet heard upon the earth and will be used increasingly by New Age groups, for the further emancipation of spirit from the bondage of fleshly limitations.

The sacred consecrational music-drama, *Parsifal*, is attuned to the same rhythmic harmonies as was the Last Supper observed by the Christ, and is a direct channel for contacting the Christian Mysteries on the higher planes of true spiritual illumination.

Wagner, an Initiate of the "Musical Ray," qualified himself as a messenger to help prepare others "to partake of redemption in advance" as he expressed it, or in the biblical phrase, to "take the kingdom of heaven by storm," both statements referring to the attainment of the Hidden Wisdom and the triumphant passage through the mystic portal of Initiation.

The Temple of the Grail, wherein this sublime music is performed, is not a poetrical phantasy about which poets dream, but an actuality within the spiritual realms. Tennyson describes it as being "built to the music of fairy harps," and Wagner says it is "located on a high and inaccessible mountain, and that the path leading thereto no human foot has ever trod."

In this Temple, Illumined Ones are working with music in relation to the further processes of man's development. There are upon the earth persons who have learned to attune themselves with the musical Ray of this Temple and consciously partake of its instruction. Richard Wagner was one of these.

Many musicians are being unconsciously influenced through its rhythms. The finer and purer the life of the musician, the more sensitive does he become to the influences emanating from this Holy Place.

The knights and maidens of the Grail are those who have been initiated into the sacred meanings and purposes of this Temple and have brought to man some phases of its truths for his betterment and ultimate regeneration. Much knowledge will be given to the world in the near future in connection with the spritual forces of rhythm.

The early Church received and used most effectually for a time much of this inner knowledge in the melodic rhythms of the Masses. Some of these were composed by the great Masters under the direct inspiration of the musical Ray of the Temple. Music has been aptly termed the handmaid of religion. Plato declared that so exalted an art was no invention of man, but a gift of the gods and was first taught to man by divine instructors.

A NEW WORLD MUSIC

The future development of the human race will be increasingly toward fellowship, unity, and equality, and the new music inspired by the msuical Temple Ray will become a tremendous factor in lifting the consciousness of man into a true perception of the real significance of fellowship, and into the realization of what a world actuated by the spirit of brotherhood as its motivating power will really mean. How glorious will be its demonstration!

A significant move in this direction has been undertaken recently by the efforts of the noted South American composer, Andre Kostelanetz, together with Jose Iturbi, the world-famous pianist, who are working unitedly on a common music form for the Western Hemisphere. As they express it, the purpose of this form is "To weld us all together into one firendly unit through melody."

Musicians have also recently observed that the music of a totalitarian world would be of a heavier and more sombre character than the light and free, rippling harmonies of the lands inspired by the idealism of free-spirited democracy.

In that supreme vision recorded in the Book of Revelation, John hears the four and twenty elders (the twelve zodiacal Hierarchies in their dual polarities) and the seven spirits before the throne (the seven planets of the solar system) chanting a new song on the coming of the Lamb. That which was new in this song was the higher pitch which each of the heavenly bodies sounded forth in its celestial symphony in consequence of that cosmic release of energy that occurred with the coming of the glorious Christ Spirit to this earth planet.

This pitch must be raised yet higher by humanity itself before the Second Coming of the Christ. Such an acceleration of planetary vibratory rhythm will take place gradually as mankind enters into an increasingly spiritual condition and brings

A New World Music

into fuller manifestation the ideal embodied in the Lord Christ. Eventually we shall have twelve planets in our solar system. The original seven have already been increased to ten and astronomers are now referring to another which is yet to become visible and to which they have given the name Vulcan. For those who are progressing along the musical Ray, future work in the Temple of the Mysteries will consist of completely musical tones of the twelve-powered zodiacal emanation. The body is destined to become veritably luminous. Man is yet to "walk in the light as He is in the light." As this state is realized, consciousness will rise to the ecstatic level of John the Revelator and like him, the illumined one will see and hear the stellar symphony, the music of the spheres.

In the words of an authentic seer, "Every nation has its soul, and every nation can find it if it will, and the soul of every people whose lineaments may be found, not in mythical gods themselves, but in what they represent—is destined to find each its altar side by side with the altars of its brother souls in the Temple of the Grail, which is the world."